THE PASTOR'S

THE
PASTOR'S
RED BOOK

WHAT YOU NEED TO KNOW BEFORE AND AFTER YOU INTERVIEW WITH THAT CHURCH

THINGS YOU DIDN'T LEARN IN SEMINARY

LLOYD R. JOHNSON

DISCLAIMER NOTICE

This book is not intended to give legal or tax advice. You should consult your legal or tax adviser regarding your situation.

Because of the dynamic nature of the internet, any Web address or links contained in this book may have changed since publication and may no longer be valid. The views expressed in this work are solely those of the author and do not necessarily reflect the views of anyone else associated with producing this book.

No part of this book may be reproduced or transmitted in any form or by any means, electronic or mechanical, including photocopying, recording, or by an information storage or retrieval system including systems not yet created without permission in writing from the publisher.

THE HOLY BIBLE, NEW INTERNATIONAL VERSION®, NIV® Copyright © 1973, 1978, 1984, 2011 by Biblica, Inc.® Used by permission. All rights reserved worldwide.

The original King James Version of the Bible is in the public domain.

ISBN 97985844900007

Copyright © 2020 by Lloyd R. Johnson, 140 Einstein Loop N Apt 21G, Bronx NY 10475-4907, USA – Email: kingdomspeaking@gmail.com or lloydatredbook@gmail.com   Web Address: www.wisdomandgodsmoney.com
Blog: http://kingsdomspeaking.blogspot.com
All rights reserved.

Dedicated to my wife
Dora M. Johnson

My children
Raymond S. Johnson & Ericka L. Blake

My grandchildren
**Ameer Blake, Bilal Blake, Nadirah Blake,
Adanne Spencer-Johnson, Na'im Blake,
Najah Blake and Zair Johnson**

Contents

	Page
Introduction	1
1. Negotiate Compensation & Tax Advantaged Benefits	3
2. Seriously Consider Secondary Income	7
3. Watchout! Especially Women	9
4. The Challenge of Dealing with the Four Types of Church Givers	11
5. Embrace Digital Church and New Things	17
6. We Saved the Best for Last	19
About the Author	23

INTRODUCTION

If You Are ... This Book is for You?

*"Commit to the Lord whatever you do, and he
will establish your plans." – Proverbs 16:3*

While working for the Board of Pensions of the Presbyterian Church (U.S.A.) as financial faculty and team member in their CREDO program, I met over 500 pastors from 2007 through 2015. They were participants in eight-day conferences our team presented twice a year. They were there to examine their spiritual life, vocational life, personal finances, physical health, and emotional health. Among other things we introduced them to *psychoneuroimmunology* = *"What one believes in his or her heart finds a place in the body."*

During those nine years I had one-on-one consultations with a little over one third. Often, we talked about more than their financial well-being. Their survival as pastors depended on these five categories working well together and finding balance. Balance does not mean equal time. If things were not well financially, for example, it interfered with their spiritual, vocational, physical, and emotional well-being. That's one of the reasons why I wrote this book. And there is Chapter 6, "We Saved the Best for Last" we hope will assist you in understanding that some of your fellow clergy see the LGBTQIA community differently than you even though you read and exegete the same Bible. I also resurrect the baptism discussion. On whom should we sprinkle, dip, dunk, or pour?

Are you a seminary or Bible college student or graduate aspiring to become a pastor? Are you a Pastor, Senior Pastor, Associate Pastor, Executive Pastor, Interim Pastor, Transitional Pastor, Lay Pastor, Temporary Pastor? Are you ordained, commissioned, licensed, or recognized as pastor by two or more gathered in His name? If you are ... this book is for you. If you are not (yet) a pastor, read it anyway so you will be ready when you get the call.

When you accept a call to pastor a church, there is more to it than applying what you learned in seminary. In addition to God's call, you are entering a vocation and becoming an employee of a congregation ... not the boss ... an employee. You may try to impress the search committee by quoting theologians like Howard Thurman or Dietrich

Bonhoeffer. You will need to convince them they are talking to the right person. As you bring ministry, spirituality, and the needs of the church, as an employee you deserve an income commensurate with your education and experience. Be assertive. You are concerned that you will have the financial resources to take care of your spouse and children. There are benefits some churches may not have thought of but are popular in the vocation of church pastor. You may have to educate the search committee and the overseeing church council. In due time you will need to refer to The Pastor's Red Book.

Believe it or not, sexism exists in the church as well as the private sector. There is still an unfounded belief that male pastors should be paid more than female pastors. And there are those who still believe women do not belong in the pulpit. We want you to be ready when prejudice rears its ugly head.

Your income is dependent on the generosity of the folks in the pew. In this book we help you understand the four types of church givers – the high-capacity givers, consistent givers, first-time givers, and non-givers, *also-known-as,* not-yet givers.

How do you and the church feel about baptisms … babies, teenagers, adults … sprinkle, or emersion? How do baptisms relate to church growth? Are you and your church on the same page when it comes to the LGBTQIA community. We help bring you closer together with healing suggestions.

If you read my book, GIVING TIME, you will notice this book is adapted from chapter 2 with input from chapters 1 and 3.

There are some things they did not have to teach you in seminary. You know you should rehearse for your interview. You know you should dress as if you are interested. You know you should smile and be pastoral and courteous. You know you should have a mentor. You know you should become a mentor. But there are some things we will share on the following pages that you need to know. While your colleagues are merely getting ready to get ready, THE PASTOR'S RED BOOK will help you get, as is says in Luke 12:35, "… dressed ready for service."

Chapter 1

Negotiate Compensation & Tax Advantaged Benefits

"Now to the one who works, wages are not credited as a gift but as an obligation." – Romans 4:4,

Your heart is beating a little faster as you hang up the phone and a smile emerges on your face. The pastoral search committee has invited you for a second interview and is looking seriously at you as their new pastor. Now you sit down and begin to recall some the advice others have given you.

When negotiating compensation with a church don't sell yourself short. They should consider your education, years of experience and any special skills you will use at the church. Determine how many hours you are expected to work. Time for sermon and Bible study preparation must be considered. That can be done at home or at Starbuck's. It doesn't have to be in the church building.

If they are not automatically part of the package, negotiate for benefits such as pension, deferred compensation, health, dental, life, disability income and long-term-care insurance … vacation, study leave and mental health breaks. In addition to salary and housing allowance, ask for Social Security Offset. *What's that?* In some churches, instead of a 1099, you receive a W-2 as a church employee for income tax purposes, but you are self-employed for Social Security/Medicare purposes (and all other non-salaried compensation) and must pay self-employment tax a/k/a Social Security plus Medicare at 12.40% + 2.90% = 15.3%. That's double what employees pay. The church secretary, for example, pays 7.65% through payroll withholding and the church pays 7.65%. Ask the church to split the 15.3% cost with you. But note: any such compensation is subject to income tax. Some denominations include this in their compensation guidelines. You might be compensated as an Independent Contractor and receive a 1099 instead of a W-2. I mention in the last paragraph of this section, your tax advisor should be well versed in clergy taxes.

When your church or denomination offers benefits, such as, pension, health and dental insurance, life insurance, and supplemental retirement savings like, 403(b)(9) and deferred compensation, take advantage of them. There are usually cost savings and other benefits with employer sponsored plans compared to acquiring them on your own. A former colleague of mine specialized in deferred compensation packages for mega church pastors. For example, a deferred comp package may include salary continuation to the surviving family for five years should the pastor die while still employed by the church. Special compensation in the event of disability is another special arrangement. Speak with a benefits specialist who understands clergy benefits.

403(b)(9) is a defined contribution retirement plan specifically designed for churches and church organizations. While similar to other 403(b) and 401(k) plans, 403(b)(9) plans are not subject to ERISA requirements, such as annual 5500 reporting. In addition, with the 403(b)(9), you can defer income tax until retirement and never have to pay self-employment tax on the amount you contribute to the plan like non-clergy employees. During retirement, you may not have to pay income tax on withdrawals if you can justify them as housing allowance and you are not using the *Roth Option* during accumulation. Under the *Roth Option,* you contribute to the plan with after-tax dollars. After age 59½ any withdrawals are tax-free. Discuss with your benefits or tax advisor about which option, *Traditional* and *Roth,* is best for your situation.

Deferred Compensation Plans are used by large congregations that can afford them. What generally happens is the church wishes to tie the pastor to the church using perquisites *(aka perks)*. Some deferred compensation plans continue the pastor's salary for a certain period beyond separation due to death, disability, or honorable retirement. Five years is a popular period of time. In the event of death, her/his salary continues to her/his family or designated beneficiary. This arrangement is often in return for the pastor agreeing to be insured to indemnify the church in the event of the pastor's death or disability. It's called key person insurance and used where there is a dynamic pastor who is responsible drawing new people and retaining existing church members tied to the church. Should the pastor die or have a long-term disability, members may decide to shop for another church. That's not the ideal situation but it happens when dealing with human beings.

Housing Allowance (HA) is a tax benefit available to clergy. It is also one of the least understood clergy benefits. According to the website www.freechurchaccounting.com, it is simply a portion of a clergy person's compensation that is so designated in advance by the minister's employing church. It benefits the clergy person because the HA is excluded from federal income tax. However, it is not exempt from self-employment tax. The employer, by official recorded action, simply splits off part of the salary and designates it "housing allowance." It cannot be more than the fair rental value of the house (furnished plus actual utilities) and must actually be spent on "providing a home." There are many resources available that describe what is eligible and what is not, based mostly on case law. (See references below to Hammar's tax guide). Also, although pastors pay self-employment (Social Security/Medicare) tax they are issued a form W-2 by some employing churches and not a 1099-MISC. Although reporting housing allowance is not required, some churches choose to report and designate it (clergy housing allowance) in Box 14 of the W-2 (which is labeled "other") as a courtesy to the pastor.

Housing Equity Allowance: Clergy who live in church-owned housing don't have the opportunity to benefit from building equity in their homes that is available to those who own their homes. This affects their ability to buy a home for retirement. For that reason, some churches will pay into an account to assist their pastor in this area. Check with a clergy compensation specialist for more information. Through google.com you will find lots of information on this subject.

I urge you to take your tax questions to and have your income tax return prepared by someone who thoroughly understands *clergy taxes*. One of the best resources is, the Richard R. Hammar – Church & Clergy Tax Guide. It has what you need to know and more. Hire a consultant to assist you with negotiating your employment contract and compensation.

Chapter 2

Seriously Consider Secondary Income

"Dishonest money dwindles away, but whoever gathers money little by little makes it grow." – Proverbs 13:11

Is the church unable to give you a well-deserved raise? Have there been hints at reducing the church's expenses by cutting back on *your* benefits, reimbursements, or your salary and housing allowance? Unless there is a dramatic change in the church's income, those things may happen. The way pastors are compensated varies from church to church or denomination to denomination.

If you are not yet a pastor, you need income. If you are between calls, you need income. Some denominations require that you jump through many hoops to become ordained, licensed, or commissioned and become a pastor or lead a para-church organization. Many pastors create passive and active secondary income. It's a good idea to choose a side-hustle you don't have to quit when a pastoral opportunity comes your way. If you love to write, magazines and blogs are looking for articles. You can write a book or a series of books. Have you thought about publishing your sermons? Do you have any specialized training? How about conflict resolution? Are you a retreat leader? A friend of mine who is a halftime pastor also leads retreats for other churches and parachurch organizations. Another pastor I know is in real estate sales. Is there room on your calendar to teach at a local college or seminary? How about coaching or consulting. There are many ways you can supplement your income with music. The list is as long, as your imagination is active. The church and your family might take up so much of your time that there is no room for anything else. Talk to a colleague who is doing it successfully.

When you are approached about leading a retreat, coaching, or consulting, the first words out of your mouth should be, "My fee is $_____." Don't be bashful about telling people your fee. You may have heard of Reverend Donnie McClurkin and Bishop T. D. Jakes, who are pastors but don't take a salary from their church. They have other income. McClurkin is a successful gospel recording artist, performer, television, and radio show host. Jakes is a successful author and produces movies and television programs. Yes, they are high profile, but this can be done at any level. Don't forget they grew into high profile.

A pastor I met recently is also a host on a Christian cable television station and interviewer on a cable talk show. I know because he interviewed me at Trinity Broadcasting studios in New York City.

Even though you may earn secondary income, you should not allow your church to pay you less than you are worth. Insist on an annual performance review so that the church and you know your effectiveness.

Chapter 3

Watchout! Especially Women

"I am sending you out like sheep among wolves. Therefore be as shrewd as snakes and as innocent as doves." – Matthew 10:16

Jesus sent The Twelve out warning them to be extremely careful. He told them to stay away from Gentiles and Samaritans. He said, "Go rather to the lost sheep of Israel." "… flogged in the synagogues." Sounds like Jesus is warning them to be wary of their own people. For us that would be our own church folks.

If you are a solo pastor, senior pastor, or lead pastor, avoid being hired as part-time. Some churches offer three-quarter-time, half-time or even less. It's because they think they can't afford to pay more. There is no such thing as a pastor working part-time. Part-time is only in the amount of money you are paid. It's not in the time you put in as a pastor. If you are hired part-time, find another church who will hire you part-time (the rest of the time). Each church will find out what part-time really means. They will compete for your time and money becomes the great equalizer. Be assertive. But, if they really can't afford full-time and you know God is calling you there, go.

Learn everything you can about the church's financial situation. Learn everything you can about the property. Are there any structural issues or major repair issues? Are there any liens of the property? Is the church being sued? Ask to see the financial statements, budget, and auditor's report for the past five years. Are the weekly tithes and offering trending up, down or is it stagnant? Are bills paid on time? Is there an endowment or investment portfolio? If yes, does the church draw from it regularly? Why? Does the church own other real estate? Is it income producing? Are more than 50% of members using recurring online giving? Does the church contribute at least 10% of its income towards helping the least among us?

Women: Avoid being short changed when it comes to getting paid what you are worth. I once heard someone say, *"We couldn't afford a male pastor, so we hired a female."* Some people in our churches have the audacity to be gender biased when it comes to paying women pastors and assigning duties … yes, in this day of awareness.

Women should apply for solo and senior pastor positions. We have noticed some churches tend to only offer female clergy associate pastor positions. When I was part of the clergy consulting team I mentioned in the *Introduction*, I recall, of the seventeen women clergy at one of the conferences, sixteen of them were associate pastors to male senior pastors. Only one was a solo pastor. She happens to be a friend, Reverend Joann White of First Presbyterian Church of Saranac Lake, New York. Reverend White could write her own book about generosity in the church. They doubled their per person giving without increasing membership.

Women must be assertive … demonstrate their value. One of the women at that conference was actually pastoring a church for no pay. The church reached a point where they had no money to pay her, but they begged her to stay. *What would you do?* She stayed because her husband, also a pastor, was earning enough for both of them through his church compensation and real estate business … that secondary income.

Become a *generosity* preacher. Avoid becoming a *prosperity* preacher, also known as *pulpit pimp*. When the focus is on money and personal financial reward, sometimes that causes us to move our thinking in the direction of prosperity. The next thing you know you'll be buying a Rolls Royce for you and one your spouse. And you will find scripture to justify using church funds for the purchase. Keep humility, generosity, and obedience in the forefront of your personal and public ministry. Members can sniff out narcissistic and selfish motives.

Lastly, let your own giving be cheerful and sacrificial and do not allow the church to be all about you.

Chapter 4

The Challenge to Dealing with the Four Types of Church Givers

"The wicked borrow and do not repay, but the righteous give generously." – Psalm 37:21

Now, I am going to present you with some challenges. The first involves members and friends of the church who give money. Here are four types of financial givers:

1. **High-Capacity Givers** – Those who give out of their assets or net worth regularly … wealthy people.
2. **Consistent Givers** – Those who give out of their income regularly.
3. **First-Time Givers** – Those who never gave to this church before. First-time givers are not necessarily first-time visitors. They may have previously belonged to this next group.
4. **Non-Givers** – Those who attend regularly but never give. I prefer to call them **Not Yet Givers**. ♪*… and we'll understand it better, by and by.*♪ We need for them to understand it better right now. They worship regularly. They even serve on committees. But they are not yet financial givers.

Some of my pastor friends and folks in the pews, are going to freak out with this next suggestion. Pastors need to know who in the congregation are the *high-capacity givers* and how much they give. Yikes! And Pastors need to know who the first-time givers are. Pastors need to know who is responsible for the church's income. Just as the pastor needs to know who in the congregation is disruptive, gossiping, is a negative force; the pastor needs to know who the positive forces in the church are. That includes, "Who gives the big bucks?" You are thinking, *"But, what people give, is none of the pastor's business."* **Yes, it is!** In addition to pastoring the church, you are CEO of a business enterprise. The difference is God the Father, Son and Holy Spirit chair your Board of Directors. You know just about everything else about your members, don't you? *"Be sure to know the condition of your flocks, give careful attention to your herds."* – Proverbs 27:23

Ask the treasurer or bookkeeper, *confidentially of course*, to tell you who are the high-capacity givers. Let them know this is just between the two of you. Ask also for the names and contact information of the first-time givers. First-time givers should receive handwritten notes from you. Explain your purpose if you feel you need to. This gets the bookkeeper working with you. You won't have to always ask. You will receive the necessary information in a timely fashion. Don't abuse this privilege in any way, shape, or form.

High-Capacity Givers: As mentioned above, these are people who give out of their assets or have much higher than middle class income. They may be business owners, professionals like doctors, successful lawyers, and corporate executives. They may be wealthy through family inheritance. Sometimes that is coupled with business ownership. They may be wealthy through their own frugality. Homeownership and a 401(k) plan have made millionaires of some people. High-capacity givers may be able to offer advice regarding church finances simply because of the business they are in.

If they are successful in business, they are up on the latest technology and will be advocates for digital and recurring giving. Being in business, they see the value. Find ways to thank them. When seeking their advice, you should offer to visit them for lunch or breakfast at or near their place of business. It would be appropriate to bring a gift, like a book or something useful. When I was working in the financial services industry, I found business owners appreciated breakfast meetings more than lunch meetings. It's at the beginning of the workday rather than interruptive in the middle of the day.

Sometimes you can avoid a special fund-raising campaign by asking the high-capacity givers to fund a costly item. Or maybe a couple of them can take care of a special situation. I have seen this happen firsthand. Should something like this occur at your church, find a special way to say, "Thank you." If you are thinking about new strategies for the church, run it by the high-capacity givers. They would appreciate being sought out for advice, and given an opportunity, to weigh in on something important to the church without being on the board. Gather small groups of them for a networking lunch. It may be worth their while to know each other and interact business to business.

Consistent Givers: Those who give out of their income are what we call the *meat and potatoes* people. These are the people who keep the church stable and the people you depend on. They are, too often, the forgotten majority. We have heard people say, "Oh, there is no need to say thank you." YES THERE IS. *"Thank you, _____. I appreciate what you did."* That is music to a person's ears. It is like a grateful hug. It is a welcomed, cool breeze on a hot sweltering night. It's money in the bank. Be consistent in saying thank you to the consistent givers. They are the ones in whom you will notice increased or decreased giving when either begins to trend. High-capacity givers are *gravy* on your *meat and potatoes*.

First-Time Givers: They never gave to this church before this past Sunday. They may or may not be first time visitors. They have been sitting in the pew for weeks. They may have been sitting in the pew for years. They brought you their problems and sought your advice. When the bookkeeper gives you the name and contact information of a first-time giver, send that person or family a "Thank you" note immediately. People like to be acknowledged and thanked. First-time givers also need encouragement. Let them know in which other areas they might serve the church. First-time givers are potential volunteers now that they have taken this giant step.

Here is an interesting tidbit. *Volunteers tend to give more than people who don't volunteer.* Increased giving and increase in the number of volunteers are tied to church growth. As the church grows, the number of volunteers grow and the giving increases. Remember that.

Non-Givers are Not-Yet-Givers: This may be a revelation to some, but they do exist. I mentioned in chapter 1, according to ChurchMag, 33% to 50% of church *members* report they give nothing at all to the church. Other statistics say it's 25% to 30%. Non-Givers have been attending your church for many years. Like Jesus, we need to look upon them with compassion. Think of them as on their way to becoming First-Time Givers. You know their faces and their names. They serve on church committees. You recognize them in the supermarket, and you greet each other with a smile.

The blog, SeedTime (www.christianpf.com), lists the following 8 Reason People Don't Give to Church:

1. Don't Have a Church Home
2. Don't Understand the Concept of Giving
3. Not Committed to the Mission/Vision of the Church
4. Bad Church Experience
5. Don't Agree with How Finances are Managed
6. Unemployed
7. Support Other Ministries
8. Think Others Will Do It

Over the years, competition for the charitable dollar has increased. There are many more charities out there. Fund raising greets you on Facebook, Instagram, and other social media. Sometimes members may disagree with a controversial decision the church has made and are withholding funds in quiet protest. Some do not know what God's word teaches about giving and generosity. So, they do not organize their budget properly.

Don't let church finances become a preoccupation. As pastor, you have a lot on your platter. Find the right person in the congregation to be the *Champion of Financial Strategy*. That's not the treasurer. The treasurer is the manager and has enough on his or her plate. The champion of financial strategy and church treasurer, together with the finance committee, get the job done. Plan, with the finance committee, stewardship committee or others, how the congregation will be educated about cheerful giving based on God's word. That group should read and understand this book. Think about these, pastor, when you prepare your next sermon and especially your sermon on giving.

Are there members of your congregation who have the talent and expertise to prepare giving talks and the technical know how to teach and help educate the congregation to become computer savvy, or provide financial literacy education?

Jot down how you feel right now and action you plan to take because you read this book. Transfer the following to your "To Do" list.

I will adjust my church compensation and benefits: _____

I will derive secondary income from: _____

Action I will take regarding the Four types of givers:
- High-Capacity Givers _____
- Consistent Givers _____
- First-Time Givers _____
- Not-Yet-Givers _____

A church's income and therefore the pastor's income depends on the generosity of its members. With our own personal finances, we work all week or all month. Then we get paid. We take the money to Walmart and buy stuff we need and want, and we go online to pay the bills.

With church finances, we tend to do things backwards. We decide how much we are going to spend next year. Usually, the pastor and finance committee or trustee board or whoever does this in your church, plan the spending on the needs and wants of the church. We plan for the giving to be 10% higher than last year. It has never happened before. Actually, income has been trending downward. But for some reason we plan for it to increase every year. Then we give each church member a box of weekly envelopes. We print the words "Tithes & Offering" in the Sunday bulletin.

There was a time when the offertory was a celebration, an integral part of worship. Today, the pastor is thinking, *"We apologize for this brief interruption. It's time for you to give God whatever money you have leftover."* But the pastor or worship leader announces, "We will now receive your tithes and offering." That is the extent of our church income planning. That must change. The pastor must initiate or have the "Champion of Financial Strategy" initiate it and the pastor whole heartedly support it.

Church leaders need to do what farmers do. First, the farmer prepares the soil. Nutrients are added if needed. Then seeds are planted *carefully*. The field is watered regularly. Weeds are pulled consistently. At harvest time the farmer reaps a bountiful harvest. If the goal was to have a certain number of bushels, that will be the number if the work was done properly and the weather was good.

If each member of the financial team including the pastor at your church were asked, *"What are the number one and number two financial goals of this church?"* Would everyone offer the same answer? Try asking at your next opportunity. That's your first goal ... to get the financial team to agree on the church's financial goals as they relate to the church's income ... not expenses.

Among your church's *financial* goals should be **Increase Giving.** On average, Christians give about 2.5% of their gross income to their church. There are those who give 10% and some give more. There are many who give less than 2.5%. Talk to members about increasing the *percentage* of their giving. While we would love for everyone to tithe (give10% of gross income), it is not realistic as a short-term goal. Short-term is what you want to accomplish this year. Figure out what percentage you give of your gross income. Pledge to give one percent more. If you now give 2.5%, increase it to 3.5% beginning your journey toward 10%.

Not everyone will increase their giving. Some people will increase by a dollar amount rather than by a percentage. Suppose only one quarter of the givers make an increase? You would still see something significant. Set a target. Would you like at least 25% of your members to increase their donations by one percent of their gross income? Announce the one percent increase goal to the whole congregation. If you don't ask, you won't get.

The announcement should be made during worship and reinforced in a sermon about money. It should also be in the church newsletter, website, Twitter, and Facebook page. Schedule a monthly Stewardship Moment or Giving Talk just before the offering. Decide who will give the two-minute talk. The pastor should preach four sermons during the year about money. One of the money sermons should be on giving. Never apologize for talking about money. Be like Jesus. *(See 3rd paragraph following this one)*

In the Stewardship Moment or Giving Talk, don't talk about fixing the boiler or paying off the church's loan. The congregation knows about that and they don't care. That's right. If their spiritual needs are being met, they don't care. *Okay, maybe they do care but there is no sense of ownership on their part*. And please don't tell them the church is broke. Nobody wants to belong to a broke church. They want to belong to a thriving church, and they will. Talk about mission and the good things the church is doing.

A short message just before the offering can sound something like this, *"It's Giving Time once again here at _____ Church. The ushers will be coming to you shortly. I want to take a moment to tell you about the new Community Pantry Ministry we are starting here at _____ Church. The pantry will distribute groceries to people in our community ... our neighbors in need. A portion of every donation we receive from you will go to assist the pantry in feeding the hungry among us. If you can increase your regular donations by just one percent, it would help a lot. Would you do that? And I want to encourage those who have never given anything to participate and give something today. Christ is counting on you. Thank you for your generosity and God bless you."* Done.

Do something similar every month. Keep track. As soon as increases are noticed, "Thank you" emails or "Thank you" notes should go out to the givers. Say, "Thank you" during worship, in the newsletter and on the website. If the pastor tweets, say, "Thank you" with a tweet. Find out who in the congregation is on Twitter.

Jesus talked more about money than anything else except the Kingdom of God. Thirteen of his thirty parables were about money. Some prosperity preachers say that is a sign Jesus wants us to be rich. Not true. Jesus talked about money and possessions because He knew money is where we would have difficulty and stray off the path. With every example, metaphor and parable about money, he is pointing us to God's kingdom. Jesus doesn't want us to be rich and He doesn't want us to be poor. He wants us to be with Him in the Father's kingdom. 1 Timothy 6:10 says, *"For the love of money is the root of all kinds of evil. Some people, eager for money have wandered from the faith and pierced themselves with many griefs."*

According to ChurchMag, an online Christian Blog and supplier of reliable church information and statistics, 33% - 50% of church members report they give nothing at all to the church. These are those who regularly attend and participate in worship, but financial generosity hasn't bit them on the bottom yet. Statistically, it could be a substantial number in some churches.

A must for churches today is online giving. Before the pandemic I asked a pastor friend, Rev. Richard Hong of First Presbyterian Church of Englewood (NJ), how congregation giving was doing. He said it was going great because over 50% of giving was online recurring giving.

If you are interested in the virtual offering plate, the Presbyterian Foundation has partnered with Vanco Payment Solutions for online giving. There is no annual or monthly fee. The administrative fee is only 2% per transaction.

Go to www.presbyterianfoundation.org/onlinegiving.

Chapter 5

Embrace Digital Church and New Things

"See, I am doing a new thing! Now it springs up; do you not perceive it? I am making a way in the wilderness and streams in the wasteland."
Isaiah 19-20

    Embracing digital church means more than preaching from your iPad. The COVID-19 Pandemic of 2019/2020 caused churches and almost all other entities that deal with the assembling of people to embrace digital media and thus digital church. Two months before the new corona virus put New York City into lockdown, a Baptist minister was telling me she had been conducting Bible study using Zoom since 2019. *What?* She is an associate pastor and a mega Baptist church in Brooklyn, NY. When New York City began to shut down in March of 2020, her church, Emmanuel Baptist Church in Brooklyn NY, had been live streaming their weekend worship services for several years. Many of their members were using recurring online giving. They were veterans at using Zoom for meetings. On the opposite end I knew of churches in 2020, who didn't even have a computer.

    Among the many members at Emmanuel are my son, Minister Raymond S. Johnson and my daughter-in-law, Nikki A. J. Johnson, my sister, Deacon Veronica P. Monro and my brother-in-law, Reverend Tyrone E. Monro, associate pastor.

    The senior pastor at Emmanuel, Reverend Anthony L. Trufant, has a philosophy, "Let's try it." He holds an annual conference for pastors and church leaders called "Rethink & Retool." It's designed to get pastor to think beyond what's happening now. The conference reminds me of the Henry Ford quote, *"If you always do what you've always done, you'll always get what you've always got."*

    What's next in the digital arena? Who knows? I am on the pulpit supply list for the Presbytery of New York City. Churches call us who are on the list when they need preachers due to vacations, illness or there is no pastor at a church. I had been preaching one Sunday a month at two churches when Covid-19 reared its ugly head. I still preach at one of them via creating a worship video. They edit the video adding the choir and other music and readings and upload it to YouTube. It premiers on their website on Sunday at 11:15 AM and it's available any time after the initial posting. I was asked to preach somewhere else one Sunday in July 2020 and found myself preaching in two places on the same Sunday morning via pre-recorded video. In addition, my own church was without a pastor. I and three other members of our congregation preach there once a month live at a Zoom worship service. One of the other members is a seminary graduate and another is a seminary student.

Live/Digital offers many options. With Live Stream, Facebook Live, Zoom, Google-Meets, etc. and video. You can preach everywhere in the world with zero travel cost. You can combine live with prerecorded.

I'm surprised every week when I observe the variety of virtual worship services churches offer. The pandemic had activated the creative juices in church leaders, business leaders and political leaders. While watching the Saturday evening virtual worship service of Alfred Street Baptist Church (Alexandria VA) on November 14, 2020, I noticed the number of views was more than 2,200. Then the next day at worship the number of views was more than 8,200 that's much more that they can fit in their sanctuary. Alfred Street had been using forms of virtual worship for several years and developing a worldwide following. They stream an extra virtual worship service on Sunday afternoons at 2:00 PM eastern time to accommodate a large following in California. By the way, Alfred Street is where President Obama and his family worshiped on Easter Sunday when they occupied the White House.

When you try something new at the church, don't be discouraged if it doesn't work well at first or if you and others stumble. New systems undergo growing pains. If it fails, as least you know after you have tried several times it doesn't work.

Chapter 6

We Saved the Best for Last

"Therefore, go and make disciples of all nations, baptizing them in the name of the Father and of the Son and of the Holy Spirit, and teaching them to obey everything I have commanded you." – Matthew 28:19

There are many things you will have to do in order to grow the kingdom. Here are two that are essential *in my opinion:* (1) Baptize teenagers and adults by emersion, and (2) Welcome the LGBTQIA community into your congregation.

I have noticed that churches that grow, also baptize teenagers and adults by emersion, and immediately engage them in learning. Baptizing or dedicating babies is important. But some parents who are not religious do not take it seriously. Parents who do not go to church or do not have a church home will telephone churches in their neighborhood and say, "I want to get my baby done." Some churches baptize babies, and some have baby dedications. The statement, "Get my baby done" covers both possibilities.

When Jesus was eight days old, he was given the name Jesus and was circumcised. *"When the time came for the purification rites required by the Law of Moses, Joseph and Mary took him to Jerusalem to present him to the Lord."* Luke 2:22

Some African cultures have baby naming ceremonies which is a grand celebration. You may recall in the novel and TV movie Roots, the baby, Kunta Kinte, was taken by his father to an open field and held up to God, and repeated the words, "Behold! The only thing greater than yourself."

The pastor and perhaps one or two officers of the congregation may meet with the child's parents before the baptism or dedication ceremony. The non-churched parents will nod their heads and say whatever they have to say in order to *"get the baby done"* and go home after the ceremony and have a party.

Thank God for the churched parents who are serious about the event regardless of whether the denomination baptizes or dedicates babies. The parents speak for the child and the child becomes a member of the family of God. In churches where the child is baptized, the child is given the opportunity to *confirm* his or her baptism later; usually around age thirteen. I believe there is rejoicing in heaven at the time of any baptism ... whether it is an adult, a child, even the child of nonbelievers.

When teenagers and young adults are baptized, become engaged in Bible study and give attention to *the least of these*, your church will grow. Now, that the church has baptized this new person in Christ, the church is responsible for teaching the new believer about Jesus and what it means to be baptized in the name of the Father, Son and Holy Ghost and become a disciple. When a thirteen-year-old claims to confirm his/her infant baptism, the teenager hasn't got a clue and is not a new believer. There is heightened excitement when a person is baptized by emersion as opposed to sprinkle or poured on.

"... make disciples of all nations." The Greek word translated as "all nations" is ethne or ethnos which can also be translated "not us" or "not one of us." And we do not have to go far to find people who are not one of us. It depends on who you define yourself to be. So, the great commission can read, *"Therefore, go and make disciples of all those who are not one of us."*

I wonder if Ephesians 4:5, *"... one baptism,"* means you celebrate your baptism only once during your lifetime or does it mean baptism has only one meaning?

When Jesus sent out The Twelve early in their training, they were not to go to *ethnos* (Gentiles or Samaritans) but to kinfolk, the lost tribes of Israel. Now he commissions them and us to go to all those who are not one of us ... all nations ... Gentiles, Samaritans, Asians, Americans, Africans, Russians, Germans, Mexicans and whoever else we find. Too many churches grow their membership by transferring members from one church to another. That is not making disciples of all nations.

Whether or not your church welcomes, baptizes, and teach members of the LGBTQIA community, will also help to determine whether or not your church is growing and headed in the right direction.

I mentioned Alfred Street Baptist Church in chapter 5. At the time of this writing, their pastor, Rev. Dr. Howard-John Wesley, hosted on his church's website and YouTube, a study series he called, "Can I Push It? – Sexuality, Spirituality, and Scripture." There are seven episodes. He interviews pastors and seminary professors who are on both sides of the question or on the fence. He says, "Sometimes, to know what you believe, you've got to know why other people believe differently ... your belief is not the only Christian position."

Go to www.alfredstreet.org/canipushit and scroll down. You will see the Promo and all seven episodes. Some of his guests are Rev. Dr. Cleotha Robertson, Rev. Canon Kelly Brown Douglas, Rev. Dr. Judy Fentress-Williams, Rev. Dr. Obery M. Hendricks Jr., and others. They represent Presbyterian, Episcopal, Baptist, AME and other denominations but they share their personal convictions. They cover the subject referencing Old and New Testament scripture and the writings of other scholars and theologians. I recommend everyone view the *Can I Push It* videos. Dr. Wesley does not try to persuade us one way or the other.

Finally, Jesus did not baptize anyone although he asked to be baptized. *What do you think of that?* Jesus had nothing to say about what we refer to today as LGBTQIA issues. *What do you think of that?*

He said, "Therefore, go and make disciples of all nations" no exceptions … everyone. He said when you, feed the hungry, give drink to the thirsty, take in the stranger, clothe the naked, take care of the sick, and visit those in prison, when you take care of the least of these brothers and sister of mine, you take care of me. And God will take care of you.

"and teaching them to obey everything I have commanded you. And surely, I am with you always, to the very end of the age." Matthew 28:20

About the Author

Lloyd R. Johnson

Lloyd joined the insurance industry in 1968 and eventually became licensed to sell all forms of insurance, a licensed stockbroker and registered investment advisor. After working for several companies, he created his own insurance and financial consulting agency, LRJ Planning Advisors LLC. He retired in 2006.

From 2007 through 2015, Lloyd was a financial faculty team member of Presbyterian CREDO, a program of the Board of Pensions of the Presbyterian Church (U.S.A.). They hosted week-long conferences for up to 35 Presbyterian pastors where the pastors examined their spiritual life, vocational life, personal finances, physical health, and emotional health. Lloyd was also active with the ecumenical Christian movement, *Tres Dias* of Fairfield County, CT.

In 2010, Lloyd completed the Commissioned Lay Pastor program with the Presbytery of New York City at Auburn Theological Seminary. He is certified "prepared for commissioned pastoral service." He is also the author of *Fools Never Raise Their Thoughts So High* and *GIVING TIME*.

Lloyd and his wife, Dora, have a son and daughter and seven grandchildren. They are members of Eastchester Presbyterian Church, Bronx NY and volunteer with Kairos Prison Ministry, Inc. ><

NOTES

NOTES

Made in the USA
Coppell, TX
06 April 2021